PEOPLE YOU SHOULD KNOW

TECUMSEH

Get to Know the Shawnee Chief Who Fought to Protect Native Lands

by John Micklos, Jr.

Consultant:
Rhonda Dass, Ph.D.
Director, American Indigenous Studies
and Museum Studies
Minnesota State University, Mankato

CAPSTONE PRESS
a capstone imprint

Fact Finders are published by Capstone Press,
1710 Roe Crest Drive, North Mankato, Minnesota 56003
www.mycapstone.com

Library of Congress Cataloging-in-Publication Data
Library of Congress Cataloging-in-Publication data is available on
the Library of Congress website.

ISBN 978-1-5435-5529-5 (library binding)
ISBN 978-1-5435-5927-9 (paperback)
ISBN 978-1-5435-5539-4 (ebook PDF)

Editorial Credits:
Mari Bolte, editor; Kayla Rossow, designer; Svetlana Zhurkin, media researcher;
Tori Abraham, production specialist

Photo Credits:
Alamy: Lebrecht Music & Arts, 5, Niday Picture Library, 13; Courtesy Chief Glenna J. Wallace,
29; Getty Images: Bettmann, 27; Indiana State Library, Indiana Map Collection, 22; iStockphoto:
benoitb, 10; Library of Congress, cover, 25; Newscom: Picture History, 21; North Wind Picture
Archives, 8, 9, 11, 15, 17, 19, 28, NativeStock, 7
Design Elements by Shutterstock

Source Notes
page 11, line 4: "Summer 1811: Tecumseh Attempts to Negotiate with White American Settlers." National Park
Service. https://www.nps.gov/articles/tecumseh.htm. Accessed 23 August 2018.

page 17, sidebar, line 5: Jim Poling Sr. *Tecumseh.* Toronto: Dundern Press, 2009, p. 62.

page 20, line 3: Adam Jortner. *The Gods of Prophetstown.* New York: Oxford University Press, 2012, p. 6.

page 21, line 4: "Tecumseh to Governor Harrison at Vincennes." The World's Famous Orations. https://www.
bartleby.com/268/8/4.html. Accessed 19 September 2018.

page 23, fact box, line 5: R. David Edmunds. *Tecumseh and the Quest for Indian Leadership.* Boston: Little,
Brown and Company, 1984, p. 154.

page 24, line 2: Ibid.

Printed in the United States of America.
PA48

TABLE OF CONTENTS

DREAMING OF UNITY

Cannon fire boomed around Fort Detroit on the morning of August 16, 1812. War cries rang through the morning air. Roughly 2,000 U.S. soldiers, under the command of General William Hull, waited inside. Outside Isaac Brock led 1,000 British soldiers. Shawnee chief Tecumseh joined him with several hundred of his own men.

A white flag rose from inside the fort. Hull had **surrendered** before the battle even began. He had more soldiers. He had the protection of the fort. Still, he feared Tecumseh and his warriors.

For most of Tecumseh's life, he had fought against white settlers taking Shawnee land. When the War of 1812 (1812–1815) began, he sided with the British. He believed they would help the tribes defeat the colonists. On this day, it looked like it could be possible.

United States Versus Great Britain, Part 2

The War of 1812 started just 30 years after the American Revolution ended. It revolved around trade and land disputes. The war ended without settling either of these issues. It was the last time the British invaded the United States.

The victory at Fort Detroit gave Great Britain control over Michigan Territory.

surrender—to give up or admit defeat in battle

ACROSS OHIO

Tecumseh was born in 1768. His people, the Shawnee, lived in Indiana **Territory**, in what is Ohio and Indiana today. Around that time, settlers began occupying Shawnee lands in current-day Kentucky. As they pushed farther into already occupied territory, they were met with resistance. Tecumseh's father was killed defending his home.

Tecumseh's brother, Cheeseekau, took over as head of the family. He taught Tecumseh to hunt. The two brothers formed a strong bond.

DID YOU KNOW?

Historic Shawnee sites have been found in the United States, Canada, and Mexico.

territory—a geographic area belonging to or under the control of a government

The Shawnee people traveled from place to place to find food.

The Shawnee

Shawnee territory originally stretched across Ohio, West Virginia, and parts of Pennsylvania. The Shawnee are an Algonquian tribe. They are closely tied to the Fox, Kickapoo, Delaware, Seneca, and Sauk tribes. Men hunted and women grew food. In the mid-1600s, they were forced from their lands by the Iroquois. They returned around 1725, but by the 1760s pioneers had begun moving west.

The Revolutionary War (1775–1783) brought white conflict across the continent. Although most major battles took place near the colonies, others spilled onto the frontier. Both the colonists and Great Britain tried to gain support from Native American tribes.

Many tribes tried to stay out of the war. For others, siding with the British made sense. In 1763 the British government had passed a law that kept settlers from traveling west. The Native Americans hoped that, if the British won, this protection would continue.

The Revolutionary War was a fight between Great Britain and the colonists. But it was also a contest for native land.

But Great Britain lost the war. In 1783 they signed the second **Treaty** of Paris. They gave up their claim to millions of acres of land across North America, called the Northwest Territory. No native people had a role in signing the treaty. The United States opened up that land to white settlers in 1787.

a map showing the Northwest Territory, 1787

THE NORTHWEST TERRITORY was divided into the five following states (with Minnesota east of the Mississippi) : 1. Ohio, admitted 1803 ; 2. Indiana, admitted 1816 ; 3. Illinois, admitted 1818 ; 4. Michigan, admitted 1837 ; 5. Wisconsin, admitted 1848. (See note on map of U. S. 1783.)

THE NORTHWEST TERRITORY, 1787
South Carolina ceded her western territory to the U. S. in 1787

SCALE OF MILES
0 50 100   200   300   400

Longitude   West   from 82   Greenwich   77

Tricky Treaties

Between 1778 and 1871, Native American tribes signed hundreds of treaties with the U.S. government. The first treaty was a military pact with the Delaware. Both parties agreed to assist each other in times of war. However, historically most of the treaties were broken when it was convenient for the government.

treaty—a formal agreement between nations related to peace, alliance, or trade

Cheeseekau trained his brother for battle. Tecumseh soon became skilled in using war clubs, bows and arrows, knives, and muskets. He was also a skilled hunter, often bringing down enough game to share with his friends and neighbors.

In 1786 the brothers left to fight the Long Knives, which is what the Shawnees called the colonizers. Tecumseh soon earned a reputation as a brave warrior.

As a young man, Tecumseh led raids across Tennessee and Kentucky.

Speak Up

Tecumseh was not only known for hunting and fighting. He was also a great speaker. William Henry Harrison described Tecumseh as "one of those uncommon geniuses which spring up occasionally to produce revolutions and overturn the established order of things."

The Northwest Territory was formed in 1787. Once 60,000 settlers lived in a territory, it could apply for statehood. Ohio became a state in 1803.

In 1790 the governor of the Northwest Territory, Arthur St. Clair, raised an army of more than 1,400 men. He hoped to destroy villages belonging to the Miami, Shawnee, and Delaware people. At first, the villagers fled. But under the leadership of Miami chief Little Turtle, they quickly organized and began a counterattack. St. Clair's inexperienced army, led by General Josiah Harmar, was easily defeated.

In 1791 the U.S. Congress found money for a second **campaign**. This time, General St. Clair led more than 1,400 soldiers. Once again, though, they lacked experience and discipline. On the morning of November 4, 1,000 members from 10 different tribes fought together. Led by Little Turtle and Shawnee war chief Blue Jacket, they surrounded St. Clair's army at dawn. Most of the white men were killed or wounded. St. Clair was forced to resign from the army.

campaign—series of battles fought in one region

The Battle of Wabash lasted for around four hours. It was a great victory for Little Turtle and Blue Jacket.

St. Clair's Defeat

Tecumseh did not take part in the battle, now known as the Battle of Wabash or St. Clair's Defeat. He led a group of scouts who were some distance from the fighting. The battle convinced Tecumseh that working together was the answer to defeating the white settlers.

Throughout the early 1790s, **skirmishes** occurred between settlers and tribal nations. Tecumseh himself led several Shawnee raids. The U.S. Army built forts to protect the settlers. Native Americans in the area found the forts threatening.

In June 1794 Shawnee Blue Jacket decided to attack supply trains coming into Fort Recovery in Indiana Territory. He hoped that, without supplies, the soldiers would leave. Some of the British forts provided Blue Jacket's men with weapons. They also promised protection. Blue Jacket led two attacks against Fort Recovery.

Losing Their Land

The Treaty of Greenville was signed in 1795 after the Battle of Fallen Timbers. It ended the Northwest Indian War and called for peace between the U.S. government and the Indians. But it also gave the United States claim to settle most of Ohio and parts of Indiana, Illinois, and Michigan. The tribes were still allowed to hunt on the land, although they no longer owned it. Tecumseh did not support the treaty, but other chiefs signed it.

Major General Anthony Wayne was put in charge of defending the fort. He built a disciplined army of more than 1,200 troops. They marched toward Shawnee territory. Blue Jacket and his men, a joint force of Miami, Lenape, and Shawnee soldiers, waited in a clearing known as Fallen Timbers.

Tecumseh helped lead an attack meant to drive Wayne's men back. Unsuccessful, his army fled toward the nearest British fort, Fort Miami. The British commander, who had few men, refused to let Tecumseh in.

The Battle of Fallen Timbers was a disaster. Disappointed, Tecumseh returned to Indiana Territory.

The Battle of Fallen Timbers was the first major victory for the newly formed United States Army. It was also the last major battle of the Northwest Indian War (1785–1795).

skirmish—a minor fight in a battle

4 A LEADER AT HOME

Back at home, Tecumseh became a war and civil chief of his small band of Shawnee. This meant that he was their leader both in times of war and peace. His village numbered roughly 250 people.

Around 1796, he married a Shawnee woman named Mamate. Together they had a son called Peekeesaa (also spelled Pachetha or Paukeesau). The marriage didn't last, and Tecumseh's sister raised the boy. Tecumseh loved his son but was disappointed when he did not grow up to be a skilled warrior.

Tecumseh moved his family several times over the next few years. Eventually they settled in what is now central Indiana. At the time, the area seemed **remote** and safe. That changed in 1800 when Indiana split from the Northwest Territory.

remote—far away, isolated, or distant

The population of the United States (which only counted white people and enslaved people) quadrupled between 1790 and 1840.

William Henry Harrison became governor of the Northwest Territory in 1798. Two years later he was also named the governor of the newly formed Indiana Territory. He encouraged settlers to his new territory. He wrote many treaties between 1802 and 1809. Those treaties gave millions of acres of Native American land to the government.

DID YOU KNOW?

William Henry Harrison fought at the Battle of Fallen Timbers. He was elected president of the United States in 1840.

A Striking Figure

There are no photographs or portraits of Tecumseh. Still, many people described him over the years. Most said he was tall and handsome. They said he had piercing dark eyes. He generally dressed in buckskin. One U.S. soldier said that Tecumseh "presented in his appearance and noble bearing one of the finest looking men I have ever seen."

In 1805 Tecumseh's younger brother Lalowithika had a vision. A healer, he watched many Indians die from white people's diseases. One day Lalowithika had a vision that his people were dying because they were leaving behind their traditions. He decided to give up the white man's ways, and began preaching about the importance of maintaining honor and their native way of life. He changed his name to Tenskwatawa, which means "Open Door." Others called him the Prophet.

Three years later, Tecumseh and Lalowithika founded a large village near the Tippecanoe River in Indiana. They called it Prophetstown. It was a religious community that welcomed people from any tribe. They could live together without the influence of white men. Tecumseh hoped that if they lived as a united community, the white men would accept them as equals.

DID YOU KNOW?

Tecumseh encouraged those in Prophetstown to give up things used by white men, such as metal cookware and alcohol.

Before becoming the Prophet, Lalowithika was not well respected among his tribe. He was not a good fighter or hunter. But his vision changed their views.

The new village worried both settlers and their leaders. Governor Harrison challenged the Prophet to prove his power. "Ask of him to cause the sun to stand still," he said. The plan worked against Harrison. The Prophet predicted a **solar eclipse** that happened on June 16, 1806. As a result, his legend grew. Word spread, and Prophetstown thrived.

Meanwhile, the number of settlers traveling west continued to grow. Harrison sought ways to get more land for the settlers. In 1809 he wrote the Treaty of Fort Wayne. More than 2.5 million acres (1 million hectares) of land across what is now Michigan, Indiana, Illinois, and Ohio would go to the U.S. government. In return, the signers would receive 2 cents an acre.

solar eclipse—a period of daytime darkness when the moon passes between the sun and Earth

Tecumseh met with Harrison in 1810. Tecumseh told Harrison that he did not agree with the recent treaties that took native land. After the meeting, Harrison wrote to the U.S. government for more soldiers.

Tecumseh, who had not been present at the treaty signing, did not accept its terms. A treaty that affected everyone, but that was not signed by everyone, was not fair. "The white people have no right to take the land from the Indiana, because they had it first; it is theirs," he said. "They may sell, but all must join. Any sale not made by all is not valid."

After the treaty was signed,
Tecumseh made a long trip.
He planned to travel among
other tribes to form an **alliance**.
He believed that the tribes were
finally angry enough to join
forces against the whites.

a map showing Indian
trails in the Ohio River
area before 1800

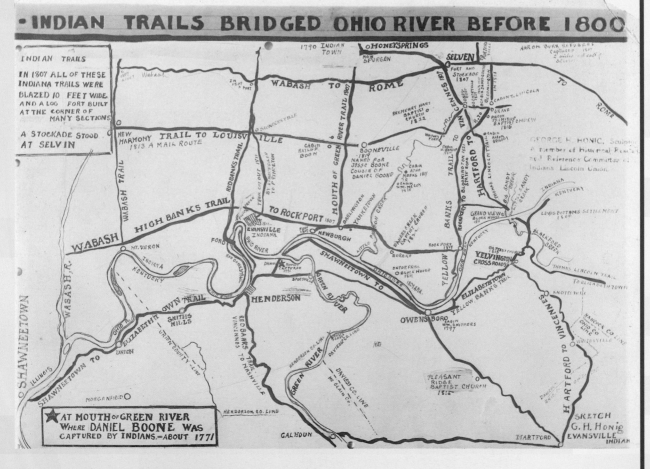

Tecumseh met with dozens of leaders between the Mississippi River and the Appalachian Mountains. People traveled from as far away as Florida and Minnesota to hear him speak. Although the people spoke different languages, Tecumseh was able to convince them that he was right. By 1810 he had formed a united front, called the Ohio Valley **Confederacy**. Ottawa, Ojibwe, Menominee, Winnebago, Wyandot, Potawatomi, Kickapoo, and Shawnee had answered his call.

While he was gone, he left his brother in charge of Prophetstown.

DID YOU KNOW?

Harrison respected Tecumseh's leadership skills. He said that if Tecumseh had lived in another place and time, "he would perhaps be the founder of an Empire that would rival in glory to that of Mexico or Peru."

alliance—an agreement between nations or groups of people to work together

confederacy—a union of people or groups with a common goal

5 THE BEGINNING OF THE END

Harrison thought Tecumseh's absence offered "a most favorable opportunity for breaking up his Confederacy." He gathered a large army. On November 6, they camped about a mile from Prophetstown.

Tecumseh had told the Prophet to avoid conflict while he was away. But his brother ignored the advice. He told his men that bullets would not harm them, and that he saw their victory. At dawn, warriors stormed the U.S. camp.

The Battle of Tippecanoe raged for just over two hours. In the end, the Prophet's soldiers were forced to retreat. The next day, Harrison's army burned the town and all the food. Defeated, the residents of Prophetstown returned to their homes.

Harrison has been criticized for attacking, rather than working with, the members of Prophetstown. The confrontation pushed Tecumseh to side with the British during the War of 1812.

Tecumseh came back to find his Confederacy broken. He and his brother and the Shawnees who remained rebuilt Prophetstown. With their food supplies gone, they struggled through a rough winter. The future looked grim.

The United States fought Great Britain once again in 1812. Allied with the British, Tecumseh and members of many tribal nations saw combat more than 40 times. Without their help, the British would have lost several major battles, including the **Siege** of Detroit in August.

In late 1813 Tecumseh had a vision of a battle gone wrong. On October 5, Tecumseh and his men were drawn into a fight with Harrison's forces at the Thames River in southern Ontario, Canada. They were outnumbered and quickly defeated. Tecumseh was killed in battle. When his men learned of his death, their spirit was crushed.

DID YOU KNOW?

After the war, Great Britain asked that land in the Ohio, Michigan, and Indiana territories be given to the Native Americans who lived there. The United States refused.

siege—an attack designed to surround a place and cut it off from supplies or help

Historians are still unsure about how Tecumseh was killed at the Battle of the Thames. Nobody knows the location of his final resting place.

LEADERS LOST

The War of 1812 was devastating for native people. Many powerful leaders had been killed. Treaties took their lands and left many without a home. When Tecumseh died, so did his dreams of a Native American alliance to stand against the white settlers.

The United States forced tribes across the country to sign more than 200 treaties. Most involved taking Indian lands. Half created **reservations** west of the Mississippi River. The tribes who lost their land were forced to move there. Some Shawnees had already moved west of the Mississippi into Missouri. Others who had remained in Ohio were moved to reservations in Kansas and Oklahoma in the 1830s. Today most Shawnees live in Oklahoma.

Fighting continued on for a year after Tecumseh's death. The Shawnee signed away the last of their land in 1817.

Tecumseh's legend continued to grow after his death. Both friends and foes respected his courage, voice, and energy. Today, towns named after him can be found across the country in Alabama, Indiana, Kansas, Michigan, Missouri, Nebraska, and Oklahoma.

Glenna Wallace was elected chief of the Eastern Shawnee Tribe of Oklahoma in 2006. She was the tribe's first female chief.

An Independent Nation

Many Shawnees have lived on the Cherokee Nation reservation in northeastern Oklahoma for decades. To maintain their identity, the Shawnees began efforts in the 1980s to separate their tribe from the Cherokee Nation. In 2000 Congress passed the Shawnee Tribe Status Act. This recognized the Shawnee tribe as a **sovereign** nation. Today there are three federally recognized Shawnee tribes, all in Oklahoma—the Shawnee Tribe, the Eastern Shawnee Tribe, and the Absentee-Shawnee Tribe.

reservation—an area of land set aside by the U.S. government for American Indians

sovereign—having an independent government

GLOSSARY

alliance (uh-LY-uhnts)—an agreement between nations or groups of people to work together

campaign (kam-PAYN)—series of battles fought in one region

confederacy (kuhn-FE-druh-see)—a union of people or groups with a common goal

remote (ri-MOHT)—far away, isolated, or distant

reservation (rez-er-VAY-shuhn)—an area of land set aside by the U.S. government for American Indians

siege (SEEJ)—an attack designed to surround a place and cut it off from supplies or help

skirmish (SKUR-mish)—a minor fight in a battle

solar eclipse (SOH-lur i-KLIPSS)—a period of daytime darkness when the moon passes between the sun and Earth

sovereign (SOV-ruhn)—having an independent government

surrender (suh-REN-dur)—to give up or admit defeat in battle

territory (TER-uh-tor-ee)—a geographic area belonging to or under the control of a government

treaty (TREE-tee)—a formal agreement between nations related to peace, alliance, or trade

READ MORE

Bodden, Valerie. *Shawnee*. Peoples of North America. Mankato, Minn.: Creative Education, 2018.

Cunningham, Kevin. *The War of 1812*. Expansion of Our Nation. Mendota Heights, Minn.: Focus Readers, 2018.

LaPlante, Walter. *Tecumseh*. Native American Heroes. New York: Gareth Stevens Publishing, 2018.

INTERNET SITES

Use FactHound to find Internet sites related to this book.

Visit *www.facthound.com*

Just type in 9781543555295 and go.

Check out projects, games and lots more at
www.capstonekids.com

CRITICAL THINKING QUESTIONS

1. How did the Shawnee people benefit from Tecumseh's efforts to form an alliance?

2. Why did Tecumseh object to the treaties selling Native American land to the U.S. government?

3. Using evidence from the text, give a few examples of how Tecumseh has become a larger-than-life figure.

INDEX